Life of a Kid

Discussion Guide

William B Elmer Jr

Table of Contents

Life of a Kid Discussion Guide

Introduction

The purpose of this Discussion Guide is to take the case Study I wrote and interpret it as a guide to raising children. This Discussion Guide may have use in other English speaking countries, but the book I wrote was written in the culture of 1930's and 1940's New England, United States. The book I refer to is "Life of a Kid". Its secondary title is "A case Study in Developmental Psychology". It is the object of this Discussion Guide. You may wish to preread the book itself. In fact it would be worth doing so in order to put yourself in the shoes of the protagonist, a slight little boy who would step away from his revelations at the age of 18. The book ends there. In almost every Chapter there are some Insights presented that will form the basis for this Discussion Guide. Prereading is not necessary, however. Your group can read a chapter a week and discuss it at that weeks meeting. There are twelve Chapters. The Insights won't necessarily be the only thing to be discussed. My own opinion is that this 13 weeks of discussion would best be monitored by a trained professional who could have many roles from peace maker to therapist. The selection of the trained professional will be dependent on the progress of the group. While the story is specific to one boy, the insights are universal.

Group progress could range from light hearted engagement in the subject matter to highly charged emotional engagement reflective of deep strong opinions by one or more group members. The abortion issue is sure to be raised. If this particular subject is broached, and I hope it will, the members are to be cautioned by the trained professional that a) this is a group that will accept all past pro-choice decisions with love, b) this is a group whose members are willing to listen to all valid arguments pro and con and c) this is a group whose members shall not be judgmental about any other group member. The trained professional will expect ALL conversations during the study to be confidential to the group and shall not be discussed outside. A commitment form might be used to get these points across.

The first Chapter, Primary Birth Imprint, covers a new concept in early childhood development. I am not aware of any such theory being put forth by any Psychologist or Psychiatrist, present or past. I therefore proclaim it as my own theory. I will explain in the next Chapter. It is important to the development of the protagonist in *Life of a Kid*. A protagonist is the leading character or one of the major characters in a drama, movie, novel, or other text. His name is Billy. Billy is me before I grew up.

If you know of any reason I should rework any part herein I would like to know about it and I cannot wait to hear from you. I can be reached at william_elmer@hotmail.com. Also, be warned, the book, *Life of a Kid*, and this Discussion Guide are Christian in nature. It assumes you want Christ to live in you and so you will find Christianity is the guiding light to some of our discussions. In other words you need to be of the Christian faith to get the full benefit of my writing.

Each Chapter of the Discussion Guide will cover a) what the Chapter is about, b) what insight it inspired in the reader and c) other possible discussion topics and then d) provide space for notes or action items.

About Primary Birth Imprint

Definition: Through nature and/or nurture, that fundamental emotional imprint through which all other emotions are processed from birth to death.

My Primary Birth Imprint is FEAR.

I wanted to give you a moment to digest that. By my definition, fear is the emotional imprint through which all my other emotions are filtered and that will be true until the day I die. Does this sound depressing? Maybe the way I have phrased it, it could be interpreted that way. But my other emotions have survived. They may be a bit weather beaten and pastel colored but I know about them and cherish them nevertheless. I found these other emotions through diligent therapeutic efforts. These efforts included one on one Psychotherapy, Men's Group Therapy, Couples Group Therapy, a Master's degree in Educational Psychology and a monumental reading program. Feel sorry for me? Don't, the Bible tells us 'And God shall wipe away all tears from their eyes.' Revelation 7:17 (NIV) My mother had Manic-Depressive disorder and finally found Lithium after 70 years of suicidal ideation and several suicide attempts on her life. Fortunately I lean toward my father's genes in this regard. He was an Engineer and mathematician. My dad and I deal/dealt with emotions by application of LOGIC and REASON.

So we know my "Primary Birth Imprint", which I shall call "PBI" hereafter. What is yours?

Note that the word "imprint" is at the heart of my definition. See Wikipedia on Imprinting of animal species: https://en.wikipedia.org/wiki/Imprinting_(Psychology) Note there is an underscore between Imprinting and Psychology. The definition of Imprinting is "in psychology and ethology, any kind of phase-sensitive learning (learning occurring at a particular age or a particular life stage) that is rapid and apparently independent of the consequences of behavior. It was first used to describe situations in which an animal or person learns the characteristics of some stimulus, which is therefore said to be "imprinted" onto the subject. Imprinting is hypothesized to have a critical period."

This occurs in all of us during the period when, as infants, we are LEARNING there are forces in our environment over which we have no control. For example, if an infant cries from hunger he learns his hunger is satisfied by receiving food and his crying stops. But suppose that his world is disrupted by a strong willed parent who wants to teach the infant to sleep through the night and does not feed the infant from midnight to 6:00 am (regardless of the cost of hearing a lot of crying.). The infant will eventually develop an emotional response. (Anger?) This response will be the beginning of the establishment of a Primary Birth Imprint. Other interactions with our infant might water down this anger. Suppose our parent in this case cuddles the infant while cooing pleasantries to him/her. Add in other emotional cues like tickling, crib mobiles, etc. For the benefit of our infant we will stipulate the parent showered the infant with a nurturing comforting love. This is a baby who will have loving as a PBI. Through this filter the baby's pale pastel anger component will be SET not to be primary for life but rather loving. This example is abbreviated in terms of duration.

So to identify ones PBI, one must consider which of ones emotions are PRIMARY. It is likely only one will be primary. Remember the properties of imprinting. It occurs rapidly. It is independent of its consequences. Suppose our infant has drawn two parents who argue a lot, are selfish and have located the infant's crib in a quiet part of the home in which they live. And, worse yet the parents do

stupid things like parrot the infant's crying, which goads it to new heights of fury. At which point father slaps the infant's bottom – hard - thinking, "There, that'll give our little troublemaker something to cry about." OR, a parent instills fear, or cowering, or withdrawal behaviors and does NOTHING to counteract and/or replace these bad behaviors which are being imprinted. No love. No respect. No exploration of the infants "personhood". Here, we have the probable outcome of a grownup who will be neurotic, or depressed or prone to spousal abuse, etc.

So now, what is your PBI? How many different PBI's might there be? This calls for input from our Discussion Group. After the discussion I will introduce a Corollary to the PBI principle.

Discussion

My PBI is:

Why do you think so?

Do I have one or more secondary Birth Imprints?

Why do you think so?

:
Enumerate all the other PBI's in the Group and are they irreducible (yes or no)?

Record some of the debates among Group members.

What question would you like to ask or insight do you want to share?

The Corollary

Now the big reveal! There are only two PBI's! All other imprints are secondary. The two are the Yin and Yang of a spiritual and emotional dichotomy. The Yin, the white in our illustration, is love and the Yang is NOT hate, but rather rejection (NOT love), the dark side of our illustration:

There are several ways to observe this dichotomy. These are all consistent. First, let's look at the whole picture. It is a symbol, that is, a thing that represents or stands for something else, especially a material object representing something abstract. The abstraction here is either the collective abstract: MANKIND or the singular: A HUMAN BEING. What follows, and it will be brief, is describing this symbol in terms relevant to this discussion. Let the symbol now represent a single infant.

Our infant can either operate on its environment OR the environment can operate on our infant. How? Why? Envision our infant as a bundle of needs, say it is hungry. It has no concept of hunger. It is its nervous system "notifying" it of a kind of discomfort we grownups know will satisfy it if it is fed. No intent, no plan, only a signal of discomfort. Now comes our symbol of love versus rejection (or not love). The infant is fed or not fed, i.e., it is going to be loved and cherished, recognized and responded to, or it is going to be "rejected", that is, ignored or put off until later. It's first experience of personhood is about to be loaded into this precious human being's mind. The very first step to becoming a person is about to be accomplished. To feed, or not to feed is a manifestation of "to love or to reject" (our symbol). No, infant doesn't know it! But it is happening anyway, it is its innate response to external stimulus.

Failure to understand the significance of a parent's RESPONSIBILITY in this regard is DIRE! The infant's development requires the kind of steering one might compare to driving a car. Little tiny corrections determine the fate of the effort. Swerving is undesirable. So, with an infant's life. Administering APPROPRIATE servanthood by a parent is crucial to establishing a well adjusted future adult. This is the most profound meaning of responsibility. The decision to have a child (or not) is indeed a weighty one. But, how many parents actually stop and ask themselves, "Am I ready, willing and able to undertake the administration of protecting my infant's personhood." Who it will become. I contend that any adult who is NOT aware of this ordinance, has been slighted in his/her training to be an adult, has a gap in his/her own personhood a parent failed to fill. FORTUNATELY, humans are adaptable to their circumstances and most times mid-course corrections suffice.

So far we have thought of our symbol as an expression of love versus rejection.(or not-love) There are significant other ways to view the symbol. Viewed as a symbol of humankind, it is more appropriate to view the dichotomy it represents as light and darkness, perfection versus sin, and God versus human. Note the progression from the lesser to the greater. Let's look at this -again, briefly.

God versus human. Said this way seems to imply conflict and, yes, man has been in conflict with God for many many centuries. But here it is used only to describe the two portions of the circle that chase round and round within that circle in a fashion Carl Jung called the "circle of eternal recurrence". But his interpretation was NON-Christian and that it implied we would return at some point to repeat our lives once again, ad infinitum. There is a more excellent interpretation. The light part represents God calling out to humanity through the perfect person, Jesus Christ. The dark part represents humanity, who for the most part is trying to flee from God aided by the forces of darkness. The interface between light and dark represents those who seek God – and those that are falling away from God. The dark side also represents the shame of mankind through original sin and its historical perpetuation. All of which can, again, be reduced to love (God is love: 1 John 4:16b NIV), the white, and rejection (as played out in Christ's Passion), the black. Thus, our symbol is perfect for us both en masse and individually.

Now, I have described my Primary Birth Imprint (PBI) as fear. I didn't say of what, What else: rejection! (And what about death, we face it every moment of our lives.) Thus, my circumstances, the construction of my personhood by my parents, have produced FEAR – of rejection, rather than LOVE. This is sad in that it makes it very hard for me to imagine God as a loving parent and it has made it very hard for me to love people. (You can read abandonment in place of rejection.) Some of you who have been brought up under loving, nurturing parents will have a hard time visualizing this category shift. Don't feel sorry for my parents or me. It produced a person able to discover the influence of the Yin/Yang symbol on my life. And here in this Discussion Guide I have been allowed to introduce you to a God that loves, unless, of course, He has already found you.

I have used the term personhood liberally here. It is crucial you understand personhood. Let's start with the definition: **the quality or condition of being an individual person.** The definition is quite nebulous because people like fingerprints are all unique. For the sake of discussion here, it refers to the **qualities** and **conditions** bestowed on an infant and its subsequent forms, baby, toddler, child, preteen, teen and adult by its parents. If our infant is brought up in a dysfunctional family, with love being CONDITIONAL, the infant is going to feel rejected. His/her personhood will falter toward the dark. On the other hand, if our infant is brought up in a loving nurturing home with Christian values, his PBI will be love, the white side of our symbol. His personhood will prosper by any measure. Personhood begins at conception. Our infant is a blank slate until it is charged with either love or rejection (fear). Thank you for slogging through this with me, now let's move on to Chapter 2.

Resources

About Imprinting: https://en.wikipedia.org/wiki/Imprinting_(psychology)
About Babies Cries: https://www.babycenter.com/0_12-reasons-babies-cry-and-how-to-soothethem_9790.bc

About Fear: https://www.bing.com/search?q=what+part+does+fear+play+in+our+lives%3F&pc=MOZI&form=MOZSBR
About Personhood: https://en.wikipedia.org/wiki/Personhood

Optional Discussion question: Is it ever too late to break down the dark "primary birth imprint" and substitute the better one?

Optional Discussion question 2: Does fear lead anywhere besides mediocrity?
(I fear I may be inadequate to x task.)
(I'm not "good" enough?)
(I fear I may be inadequate in all things!?)
(I fear failure.)

Optional Discussion question 3: What are the implications of "primary birth imprint" on later adult and sexual development?

Optional Discussion question 4: Has God called you to do something for which you feel inadequate? Ask for God's help to rely on His divine power. -Bill Crowder of Our Daily Bread Ministries

Other optional Discussion questions:
    Do birth imprints lead to later dysfunctions or cravings?
    Is there a dysfunctional "primary birth imprint" that dooms a child to multiple divorces?
    What does conditionality of love do to human development?
    Discuss the havoc wrought by conditional love.
    When a mother says, "I hate you" to her son. Can one "I love you" undo this?
    What do demeaning behaviors do to child development?
    What do open rancor, passive-aggressive behaviors and physical abuse between parents do to child development?
    What causes social anxiety disorder?
    Discuss the importance of inculcating correct values.
    This includes the special case of the Christian faith.

Nota Bene! This course is designed for 13 weeks. Discussions about each Chapter could take **much** more time. If there is time available, feel free to make this "course" open ended!

Other Notes

Chapter 1 – My Dad – BillSr

Insight from the book: *Where there is a member of the family who has lead an exemplary life, hang on to them for dear life. Identify, realize and appreciate the goodness they bring to the family. Emulate them, don't disparage them. They can be identified by the loving patience they show. They can be identified by the respect they have for their children's and grandchildren's dignity. They love well. In this case it was Garmy.*

How can we identify such a family member earlier when we realize at age 70 they are gone?

What does this say about BillSr?

Why would one disparage such a family member?

Which is more desirable? A parent that disparages, uses passive-aggressive behaviors and teases or a parent that disciplines in love and explains carefully and in appropriate detail why punishment may be necessary in the future?

What influences on Billy's Personhood can be seen from this Chapter.

What ideas does this give you for raising children and cultivating their personhoods?

What question would you like to ask or insight do you want to share?

Chapter 2 – Aletha to Cathleen

Insight from the book: *In the case of a pending divorce, parents owe their children an honest explanation of what happened to their Covenant of marriage. Since it takes rational thinking to be able to negotiate an explanation such as this, it holds out the possibility of a reconciliation. This makes an explanation to the children doubly valuable. It would also be valuable to encourage a couple in these circumstances to engage the services of a Christian counselor. Church Ministers take note.*

How could or why should the children of a pending divorce be brought into the "matter"?

If the children are not brought into it, what are the consequences to the children?

Is there a negative effect on their personhoods?

Is this a good time to practice the "empty chair" technique?
The empty chair technique is a **Gestalt Therapy** technique where the client engages in a role-played conversation with an imagined person. The patient sits facing an empty chair, and imagines that a family member or some other specific person is sitting there.
Resource: http://www.psychologicaltechniques.com/empty-chair-technique/

Should the Covenant nature of marriage be brought into the discussion?

Change of Subject. What was the "challenging assignment" given to Billy in this Chapter?

If you were Sil's sister at that time what would your advice have been if you had been asked?

Where did Billy learn self reliance? At what age?

In what ways was Billy's personhood being developed?
    Haphazardly?
    No thought about personhood?
    Did Billy find relief to be out from under BillSr's punishment method? (The divorce)
    How did Billy come to learn to keep things to himself?
    Is the concept of personhood important?

Suppose "custodial arrangements" were not explained or discussed with Billy (8 years old) or Teddy (4 years old).
What thoughts do you have about explaining what "things" mean to your children?

Billy was confronted with endless questions by Syl and BillSr about their opposite numbers when he would get back from a visit. What strategy did he invent to combat this?

Did this influence his personhood in some way?

What question would you like to ask or insight do you want to share? Questions about Aletha maybe?

Chapter 3 – BillSr's Peregrinations

Insight from the book: BillSr struggled with the "illogic" of Jesus Christ all his life, even though his mother was a Christian. He was at one point an Odinist, feeling the logic of Odinism was unassailable. At a more recent time, he accepted the pantheism of the Unitarian Universalist "Church", a sort of modern Odinism. In his spiritual wanderings, he could not bring himself to believe in what his mother believed, yet, in an ironic twist of "fate" his three sons would all adhere to her model of accepting and loving Jesus Christ. Therefore, if you want your children to know the one true God and grow up to accept His Word, the Holy Bible, as their guide to daily living, introduce them to the Christian Church and they will learn to live a Holy life. In the last few minutes of BillSr's life he was saved by his granddaughter-in-law Cynthia P Elmer.

What kind of mind has trouble accepting the Truth about Jesus? Does the life of BillSr reveal an answer?

What strategies can be applied here to foster and encourage salvation of a loved one?

What crises did BillSr face in his life?

What makes BillSr vulnerable to Sil's passive-aggressive behavior?
(the *Diagnostic and Statistical Manual of Mental Disorders* (DSM) revision IV describes **passiveaggressive personality disorder** as a "pervasive pattern of negativistic attitudes and passive resistance to demands for adequate performance in social and occupational situations.")

What influences on Billy's Personhood can be seen from this Chapter?

Did BillSr have a passive-aggressive "streak"? We know he was disparaging of his mother. That would be a vector.

What was different about Cathleen as compared to Sil or Aletha? (Start with age)

What did Cathleen do, in the end?
    Abandon BillSr?
    Reject BillSr?
    What happened to their love? (Lust?)

What does Billy mean, his brother Ned should have been the brother to hate?

What influence did BillSr's threats to harm him financially? Why did BillSr do this?

What question would you like to ask or insight do you want to share?

Optional Discussion Question: How does a child learn how to handle being told by his father that he walked in on his second wife (not the son's mother) fornicating with a former neighbor? (male)

Resources

Passive-Aggressive Personality Disorder: https://en.wikipedia.org/wiki/Passive-aggressive_behavior

Chapter 4 – My Mom – Sil

Insight from the book: *As you can see, there was nothing whatsoever spiritual about the Elmer household. God was utterly absent. The "God" of this household was BillSr. He ruled the family with an iron hand in a conditional loving manner. That is, when you pleased him. Certainly that love evaporated when you displeased him. Sil, in her way, ruled the family the same way, but with a different technique. In no case, none, did they rule the family as conservators of two dependent children. Here the word conservator involves the qualities of unconditional love, respect, dignity and spiritual responsibility.*

What damage, and how extensive. to a child's personhood can a Godless household be?

How can the damage be rectified? Can it ever be?

What other qualities might the high functioning "conservator" of children demonstrate?

If development of a child's personhood is such a weighty responsibility, why is it ignored in books on parenting?

Just think. How can a child born into conditional love, low or no respect, no dignity and without God be nothing but dysfunctional? What hope does such a child have for being a leader, a speaker, a motivator, and a success as a father and employee?

Did Sil's childhood prepare her for marriage?

Did Sil have indulgent parents? If so, what was called for?

What does the age difference of a 29 year old male and a 19 year old female portent for a marriage? Is this a failure of BOTH sets of parents (think personhood)?

Should marriage counseling be mandatory for such age differences?

Do you suppose Billy learned from this that violence toward women was OK?

What question would you like to ask or insight do you want to share?

Resources

https://en.wikipedia.org/wiki/Beginning_of_human_personhood
https://en.wikipedia.org/wiki/Personhood

Chapter 5 - Sil's First Time as Head of a Household - 1940 – 1942

Insight from the Book: *Fear of punishment, including emotional punishment, creates a child who will refuse to trust a parent. There is a way around this. Do not instill a fear of punishment of the child. Punish the sin. If Billy uses a bad name for a bodily function, there needs to be a discussion about what we are inappropriately learning from our parents and others and how we are using that language. Your child is bound to hear swearing and misuse of grammar. Your intervention needs to be loving and focused on the sin, not the sinner. Reward whenever possible. To not acknowledge a child's sin is to give permission to engage in it.*

The highlight of this Chapter is the rainy, dank, dark morning of Sil's realization she was alone and responsible for two children, i.e. a "Head of the Household". She was truly on her own. A weeping mother and her two silent children sitting across from her in the living room. What entry was being made into the personhood "logs" of Billy and Teddy?

How does helplessness affect a family and it's members. As a group. And individually?
    Consider Sil had two living parents, two sisters and one brother.
    Aunt Virginia provided protection until the alimony started to come in.

How did the family finally rescue Sil?

Regarding the Yin and Yang symbol, what was the interplay of forces: Light v dark, Good v evil, God versus sin and Love versus rejection (or Love versus fear)?

Speculate on what in Billy's personhood might have brought him to explore his environment; e.g., Harvard University campus. Could a negative entry in his personhood "log" have produced a productive result? Can that happen?

Nightmares can be engendered by trauma. What might have engendered Billy's nightmares?

Billy came down with asthma at age four. Every Friday night he would have an attack.

Thinking of the Yin/Yang symbol, make that the basis of your answer. Why the asthma?

The asthma became life threatening around the time of the nightmares when Billy was nine. Why?

Billy developed a strategy to deal with his nightmares. What strategy did he employ in defense of his humiliating slaps by Sil?

How did Billy handle Sil's smoking and drinking? (It's not in the book.)

Does ALL fear reduce to fear of DEATH?

What question would you like to ask or insight do you want to share?

Chapter 6 - Life begins at Howard – 1941 – 1942

Insight from the book: *I believe my mother's genital display was entirely without redeeming merit tantamount to child sex abuse. If she was trying to silently supplement her earlier explanation of human reproduction, she failed miserably. I know Sil felt a lack of confidence to explain reproduction. That was obvious. This experience highlights the absolute necessity for a designated parent to explain reproduction in understandable terms that is age appropriate. Dr Bing can help with this. Importantly, choose a methodology which takes into account respect, dignity and love for the child participant.* https://www.bing.com/searchq=explaining+reproduction+to+children&pc=MOZI&form=MOZSBR

Was Sil adrift? What survival strategies (if any) does it seem she employed?

What mistake did Sil make in her attempts to provide Billy with sex education?

What are the dynamics of the "lost donuts" story. (e.g., why did Sil have to affix blame external to herself)

Why didn't she blame Teddy?

What were the dynamics of Billy's stealing the comic book? Answer in terms of personhood.

What were the dynamics of Billy accusing a schoolmate a "nigger"? Answer in terms of personhood.

What were the pluses and minuses of Sil offering Billy's services to Dr Hinton?

How must have Sil felt toward finding Howard? (now the age thing goes in reverse! Sil is 29 and Howard is 22)

I cannot remember Sil explaining what finding Howard meant to her, Me and Teddy. Be Sil and talk to the empty chair!

How did Billy know how to be neutral, non-disclosing and reticent about visiting one parent and being questioned about it by the other? Did he see it as a tool for torture, or was it inspired by the Holy Spirit?

What question would you like to ask or insight do you want to share?

Other Notes

Insight from the book: *I want to repeat what I wrote in this Chapter of "Life of a Kid" to emphasize what I had to say about love: "Where do little kids find the words to express such feelings? They need a parent's help. A sort of pre-birds and bees talk. To a parent who would nix this idea, I would say, "Then you will miss the single biggest opportunity you will have to teach the highest value, LOVE, to your child." I missed that opportunity and even regret it today, for even though I moved on from sweet Joan, I would have a crippled understanding about love for much of the rest of my life. It is crucial to note here that love as used here means genuine romantic love – not lust – Biblically as in the Book of I Corinthians in the Bible: "1 Corinthians 13:4-8: 4Love is patient, love is kind. It does not envy, it does not boast, it is not proud. 5It does not dishonor others, it is not self-seeking, it is not easily angered, it keeps no record of wrongs. 6Love does not delight in evil but rejoices with the truth. 7It always protects, always trusts, always hopes, always perseveres. 8Love never fails. But where there are prophecies, they will cease; where there are tongues, they will be stilled; where there is knowledge, it will pass away. -New International Version, Copyright 2011-2017 Biblica*

How does Sil (or BillSr for that matter) prepare Billy and Teddy for a life of frequent moves? With some kind of "Do as I say, not as I do" statement?

So, what should Sil or BillSr have been concerned with?

How does Sil (or BillSr for that matter) prepare Billy and Teddy for a life with one parent living 1/3 of the way across the United States (and even more moves)?

How does Sil (or BillSr for that matter) prepare Billy and Teddy for integrating them into a dozen varying home sites?

Do you see a common theme here? (It involves parents as counselors to their children)

Have you prepared your children for encountering their life events?

Lets list some typical life events.

Did you include puberty?

Are you prepared to discuss sex? (Time for the empty chair?)

What question would you like to ask or insight do you want to share?

Other Notes

Insight from the book: *When discussing your child's behavior with the other parent, there is NO justification for denigrating your child in order to "make yourself look good". Then, worse yet, in an attempt to set my feelings against Howard, she relayed to me what would have been a denigrating statement by Howard. Sil specialized in this "take no prisoners" mentality. This spinning of conversation to enhance ones self image is really self immolation to an aware partner.*

Billy suffered from a case of Athlete's Foot from the YMCA. Sil told Howard, who commented, "I didn't think he was enough of an athlete to have Athlete's Foot". Then Sil, at the height of cruelty, tells me what he said.

What was her motivation? How might this have affected Billy's personhood?

Like so many occasions before, Billy did not speak up, but "sucked it up" having learned the value of not being self disclosing. How can we get Billy into a safe zone where self disclosure is OK? Let's look at self disclosure first. "Self-disclosure is a process of communication by which one person reveals information about himself or herself to another. The information can be descriptive or evaluative, and can include thoughts, feelings, aspirations, goals, failures, successes, fears, and dreams, as well as one's likes, dislikes, and favorites." - https://en.wikipedia.org/wiki/Self-disclosure

NOTA BENE!!!! - Personhood is obviously a foundational concept in our discussions.
NOW WE HAVE A SECOND FOUNDATIONAL ELEMENT: SELF DISCLOSURE!
Parents all over complain their children never talk about themselves. Who is at fault?
THE PARENTS!!! The children have spent the time from ages 0 to 17.99 protecting their personhood from negative influences from their parents. Every parental BOOBOO is logged in as a negative input to a child's personhood. They are really good at this!

What can we parents do to protect our children from such parental booboos? Remember it is a boob that makes booboos. First of all we should explain in an age graded way that we parents are imperfect. We should be sure to apologize when we make a mistake. List some common mistakes parents make in their communications with their children. The big ones only please. We have some time constraints.

The List

Now our children see we are faulty, we can see how crucial it is to have high quality communication with our children. REMEMBER: Jesus was the only perfect person! We see the importance of self-disclosure. When we see the importance of self disclosure and practice it, our children find we are not perfect and join in the practice of disclosing. We now have a communicating family. Caution follows: At birth there is definitely a two way (but nonverbal) communication system between infant and parents. As the infant begins to be able to reason (however flawed!) the communication is from superior (parent) to inferior (child). But then the communications begin a lengthy process to morph into PEER to PEER. Ultimately the roles may be reversed. Here is a crucial nexus! When the first glimmer of ability in the child to speak about a subject cogently, the parent needs to be able to adapt (hopefully proudly) to the peer to peer kind of communication. The parental role most begin to become specialized as well as sparser and sparser. This is the time to begin sex education, for example. https://en.wikipedia.org/wiki/Social_penetration_theory

How might we commence communication with our children about self disclosure?

What risks may there be? (Try with your spouse.)

Let's move on. Billy showed an interest in band and was going to choose drums. In Winchester, Billy took piano lessons. Moving from place to place nixed the idea of having a piano. Any music interest withered and died when the Band Director in Minneapolis kicked me out of the initial meeting when I caught a football thrown in my direction. Did this present an opportunity for parental intervention with the school. Yes or No. Why?

Did Teddy and I need to learn about goosing at age 12 and 8 respectively?

Why didn't Billy write to Joan Jensen, Billy's first love, or Mr. Bolster, his seventh grade math teacher?

The great FALSEHOOD. "I am confident of my competence". Adapting to my mother's acting skill, I would spend much of my life imitating people who had some skill I needed. In fact I would successfully act out that behavior even though I KNEW I might fail. I might fail because it was not me carrying out the action but the other person. I was only ever, I believed, the GREAT IMITATOR! When presented with a seemingly impossible task, I would imitate my way through it. We call that utilization of models to achieve successful behavior. Everybody does it. EVERYBODY. It's just that no one ever told me that, ever. I was in my early twenties before a glimmer of that idea would sift through my conscious life. So, what part of the Yin and Yang circle was I operating under?

Why did Sil tell her story about peeing down the side of the house to all who would listen? (As an actress she could hold any audience spellbound.)

What question would you like to ask or insight do you want to share?

Other Notes

Chapter 9 – Terre Haute – High Land

Insight from the book: *One. I can assure you, your thirteen year old child will be approached for sex. I don't really need to say much more than that. Avail yourself of skilled help to prepare your child for this. I must have been prepared, but I cannot for the life of me figure out how. I imagine Dr Google will, once again, be able to ride to the rescue. There are two categories here. The physical attack of a rapist on a child. That is not what I am talking about. I am talking about a psychological "attack" which can come under another name: "grooming". Attempted grooming was used by males on me countless times! I seemed to resist reasonably well because I never alienated the one who approached me. We would remain friends. I never received any special wisdom about this except that sex was to be between a man and a woman. To be man and man was really quite laughable.*

Two. This whole department, the Insight department, was brought about by the one concept that slammed me across the bridge of my nose with a two by four. Personhood. I have expounded on it elsewhere herein, but I have to be really clear about what a valuable concept it is for parenting. You have created a child. He/she is not you. You and NOT you will be negotiating a life together starting on the day of birth. You MUST respect this division of personalities or you will literally ruin this precious other life. By now you have had a few glimpses of how true this was for me. This does not negate Tough Love. In fact it may be required at times. But as long as your love is unconditional, your respect for the child's dignity is complete and you have promulgated his/her education with Christian principles, you will have transcended the most difficult terrain in all of child rearing.
"Tough Love: Bill Milliken, Char Meredith, Bruce Larson". Amazon.com. Retrieved 2016-12-09.

This Bing response is important: https://www.bing.com/search?
q=When+others+approach+your+preteen+for+sex&pc=MOZI&form=MOZSBR
But your church is the best place to start. Just know this: Your preteen's friends, adults at certain venues like the YMCA, the kids in Boy Scouts including the camps, will interpret your child's friendly disposition as an invitation to have sex!!!! The nine to twelve age group is 100.000% vulnerable to these interactions. Prepare your child! Being social at this stage is like saying, in a cheery voice, "Hi, I'm available for sex". I mean to lay this out in NO uncertain terms. Even when I had teenagers, I did not have the sophistication to deal with this. Prepare now. ALL of these interactions I had were HOMOSEXUAL!!! To illustrate, my junior high school principal was grooming me at one point.

I seemed to have had some innate protection against this onslaught. It can only have been the Bible and the Holy Spirit.

OK. To be forewarned is to be forearmed.

Sil never emerged from the talking down to stage of communication. I could hear echos of her parents talking to her saying things like, "Oh look at 'Silia. Isn't she cute?" or "You make such wonderful mud pies, they taste so yummy, deah!", etc. Only trouble is they would dole out this kind of affirmation when she was 16 years old. So, where do you draw the line at talking down to your children?

Bill (we will now treat him with the dignity his age calls for.) like many other adults was never allowed to emerge from this stage. His solution was to stay far away from his mother, forever. How might he have interceded and brought about a restoration? (Beware!)

What were the consequences of Billy's being non-disclosing there in Terre Haute?

Bill's personhood took some major hits from Sil as soon as he started dating. How did Sil's reference to Carolyn Sutch as "Carolyn Clutch" play into the personhood matter?

Back in the Chapter where I disclosed the Corollary about Primary Birth Imprint, I said "Our infant can either operate on its environment OR the environment can operate on our infant." In the Chapter where Sil's slap has zero effect on Bill, you got the first glimmer of Bill's first reversal of the operation concept. Bill's response was him gloriously operating on the world. Then in high school we get additional but WEAK glimmer's of his operating on the world. He did not take charge of ALL areas of his life until he accepted his first career assignment. That was miserably and pathetically too late! WHY!!!

Stress insinuated itself into Bill's life for the first time in 1943, when in Norfolk, Virginia, Sil had to take Bill to the doctor to find out why a 50 cent piece sized bald spot appeared on his scalp. It was diagnosed as Alopecia areata. There is no known cause – other than stress. At age 52 it would painlessly ravage his entire body – completely! Bill was fortunate in a way. Here was an outward warning sign of inner turmoil. Sil and the doctor were helpless to help. It was all up to Bill. But was help available outside of Bill?

What question would you like to ask or insight do you want to share?

Chapter 10 – 216 Barton Avenue

Insight from the book: *This was the stage of my life where there seemed to be no resources to renew my understanding of human sexuality and at my age I could have used some guidance. Well, one exception, "Bill, don't make any babies!!" As brief a guideline as it was, it did cover a lot of ground. I did a lot of kissing though. I needed a loving discussion about sexuality. But the combination of my continuing to be non-self disclosing and my parents' remaining unwilling to talk about difficult things forbid having an open, honest and loving discussion which I needed very badly. Like, "What do I say if Carolyn asks me if I love her?" Never in a thousand years would I ask Sil that question. It's too bad too. There are many questions and many answers. Dr Google offers some help here too – not all is applicable to YOUR child, so be discerning!*
https://www.google.com/webhp?ie=utf-8&oe=utf-8#q=situations+should+I+warn+my+preteen+child

Know this: The most likely sexual predator you child will encounter is not a middle age freak! It is a male friend. How vulnerable can a child be? Have you the kind of relationship with your children that prepares them for this? (DO NOT POO POO THIS!!!!) I have laid the groundwork for you. How will you begin?

Have you considered your first sexual experience as a predation? (Think honestly now.)

Think outside the box! (i.e., add ones you doubted would qualify.)

Are not ALL sexual experiences predatory?

Can there be any non-predatory sexual experiences? (ones where both partners are willing.)

Who do you seek out when you are confused about some aspect of your life?

Consider Bill's operating on the world. It was sporadic and seldom disclosed. Give one example from Chapter 10.

Give one example of Bill's world operating on him.

What question would you like to ask or insight do you want to share?

Other Notes

Chapter 11 – The Rest of the Story

Insight from the book: *At the risk of repeating myself, have enough respect for the unique person your child is to recognize valid feelings. If you develop trust in the parent – child relationship, as opposed to fear, these things will add valuable building blocks to their ultimate purpose, their telos. Your assignment, should you accept it, is to unfailingly respect your child and his/her dignity – and help him/her find his/her telos*

A telos is an end or purpose. https://en.wikipedia.org/wiki/Telos_(philosophy)

The Wikipedia entry is incomplete. It is made complete by the inclusion of God. As the loving creator of all of humanity, He has a goal or purpose for us all. Our parent's and our life's work is to discover our telos. This is why telos is such an important concept for ALL of us. It explains why, especially to the Catholic faith, abortion is wrong. It is always wrong, yes, NO exceptions! NONE, period. In fact the Church holds that a voluntary abortion brings automatic self excommunication!!!!!!!!!!!!

Now before you here who may have had an abortion, are worried you may be hell bent, think about this: Is this not a matter of a flaw in the development of your personhood? That is a really really open ended question! Let's see how you would answer it. GO!

So, I hasten to say this: EVERYONE IN THIS ROOM IS FORGIVEN!! Breath easy now. And why are you forgiven? (assuming you have opened the door to Jesus and invited him in by confessing your sins and asking for his protection by guiding your life. If you haven't, DO IT NOW. Praise the Lord!) Being forgiven, NO GUILTY CONSCIENCES ALLOWED HERE! Can you NOW readily agree with me you are forgiven? Do you have any reservations? Speak of them now!

We've just been, for a few in this room, through a gut wrenching experience. So now let us move on to some other questions about Chapter 11. Was Bill prepared for the various moral issues that fell in his lap in High School?

Remember, Bill's personhood contained these elements: non-self disclosing, being guided by other's behavior, ill-prepared for moral challenges. How else might he be unprepared?

The Boy Scouts, that VICTIM of political correctness. Bill points out it is not so sacrosanct an organization as conservative orthodoxy and the Eagle Scouts of this land would have us think. Where does your opinion fall in a scale of one to ten, ten being a squeaky clean perfectly wonderful entity?

What property of a personhood determines its moral telos? (This is a VERY heavy question)

What other property might the concept of personhood include?

Must provision be made for ALL these?

What question would you like to ask or insight do you want to share?

Other Notes

Chapter 12 – Teddy

Insight from the book: *Teddy himself*

This Chapter is in two parts presenting reminiscences by Bill and Ted about Ted. This is an optional discussion Chapter. We could each select a paragraph and critique it in terms of personhood, self-disclosure and telos, or call it a day.

We could also discuss some of your child experiences in those same terms.

List any comments or criticisms you might have.

List anything that I missed and should have included.

Other Notes

Final Thoughts

Can you define Primary Birth Imprint?

Can you define Marriage Covenant?

Can you define Personhood?

Can you define Self disclosure?

Can you define Conservator in the sense in which we used it?

Any other key concepts you commend to future readers?

www.ingramcontent.com/pod-product-compliance
Lightning Source LLC
Chambersburg PA
CBHW081137280526
45787CB00007B/3115